Midnight THOUGHTS

ASTRID

BlueRose ONE.com
Stories Matter
NewDelhi • London

BLUEROSE PUBLISHERS
India | U.K.

BlueRose ONE.com
Stories Matter
NewDelhi • London

For permissions requests or inquiries regarding this publication, please contact:

BLUEROSE PUBLISHERS
www.BlueRoseONE.com
info@bluerosepublishers.com
+91 8882 898 898
+4407342408967

ISBN: 978-93-6261-528-2

Cover design: Tahira
Typesetting: Tanya Raj Upadhyay

First Edition: July 2024

Dedication

To all the night owls and open-eye dreamers whose minds come alive under the twinkling stars and the gentle embrace of the moonlight, this book is lovingly dedicated to you.

Preface

"Midnight Thoughts" is a collection of poetry born from the depths of these nocturnal musings. Within these pages, you will embark on a journey through the labyrinth of the human experience, exploring themes of love, loss, longing, and the enigmatic mysteries of existence. Each poem is a whisper in the night, a fragment of emotion captured in verse, inviting you to delve into the hidden recesses of the soul.

These verses are not merely words on a page; they are windows into the heart of the poet, bearing vulnerabilities and truths that resonate with the shared experiences of humanity. From the raw intensity of unrequited love to the quiet solace found in solitude, "Midnight Thoughts" seeks to illuminate the myriad facets of the human condition, offering solace to those who wander in the shadows of their minds.

As a kid, I tried to lose the flaws

they pointed at,

As an adult, I'm trying to lose the words they

imprinted.

I didn't heal,

I just stopped waiting for someone to save me.

Some people drain the nice right out of you,

till mean is the only way you can be.

There are 365 days,
There are 12 months,
There are 8,760 hours,
There are 525,600 minutes,
There are 31,536,000 seconds,
And all I did was survive.

I've never seen sparks so pretty as in the eyes of a child, Who had dreams to aspire, to become someone, someday.

I've never seen sparks die so quickly as the child,

Who grew up was told her dreams made her too much to handle.

Now she's living on survival skills,

While her demons play truth or dare in her head.

How do I go about believing in an entity I've never seen?
When the people I've grown up seeing were nothing but monsters.

I'm tired of asking myself why,
I'm tired of feeling like I don't belong,
I'm tired of holding on to pain,
I'm tired of dreaming without flight,
I'm tired of carrying this weight,
I'm tired of tears that never dry,
I'm tired of pretending to be strong,
I'm tired of the battles I've fought,
I'm tired of echoes in my head,
I'm tired of hoping for a sign,
I'm tired of false hope,
I'm tired of false what- ifs,
I'm tired of reaching for an end,
I'm tired… just tired, in the end.

I think my heart has a special chamber
reserved for Grief, a sort of a prison.
And my mind is a regular visitor.

They weren't lying when they said practice
leads to perfection,
Because now, every time someone asks me how
I am doing,
I immediately manage to plaster a fake smile
and reply with confidence,
"I'm fine"

They say it's fine to feel good about yourself,
But which 'YOU' should you be okay with?
The one you changed to please others
Or the one who's tired of always trying to
make others happy?

We are but shells of who we used to be,
Echoes fading in the sands of time's decree,
Once vibrant souls, now weathered by the sea,
Lost in the depths of life's relentless spree,
We are but shells of who we used to be.

A year can change a person,

A month can change feelings,

A week can change perspective,

A day can change the path,

But a minute can destroy everything.

I ask myself every night,
"Why do some people adore the moon?"
And the more thought I put into it, the more I understood the adoration for something full of flaws yet so beautiful, in every shape, every phase, every color, and every phase. The moon is unapologetic for how it appears, and maybe, that's how people want to be, want to feel, want to live.

*When all the noise in my head silenced,
I realized I was truly alone in a world that no
longer felt like home.*

I don't know what to say when I'm asked to
speak in a Room full of people.
Because I always live inside my head;
Visualizing scenarios and having internal
conversations,
Not everyone can digest.

There's a vulnerability in seeking help,
In exposing our innermost struggles to another person, We reach out, hoping for understanding, support, Perhaps a path towards healing,
But sometimes,
The hands we grasp for support are the ones,
That push us further into darkness.

We crave for things we never had,

Maybe that's why I craved peace.

I saw a video that said our hearts retain memories,
I'm worried whether mine is intact to hold onto memories.
And even if it does, what does it contain?
Because every time I think of my heart,
It hurts me to feel nothing good.

Wash away the horror,
That's settled in my mind,
Take away the fear,
I can no longer hide.

I sit down by the window,
Sipping on a cup of coffee,
Watching the rain pour,
Hoping nature has someone to hold it too.

There is a darkness in me that craves violence,
But the pain in me doesn't want to create my own victims.

My highs are too high,

And my lows are too low,

I'm still searching for a middle ground to

hold on to.

Most days I'm merely existing,

But the days I'm truly living,

Are the hardest,

Because I know what happiness feels like,

And I know I can't hold onto it forever.

I go to therapy weekly,
And pour out all the stories,
Of everyone that I've met and those that left.
But then it dawned on me,
Why am I here when they broke me?
Why am I paying for something they did?
Why am I fixing what they destroyed?.
Wouldn't it be better if they were here,
Instead of me?

How do you know who really loves you?
When everyone wants to change something about you,
To fit their picture of 'perfect'?
~I wish perfect wouldn't come with the cost of losing myself~

I don't think I'll ever know love beyond family,

Because every time I think they will stick around,

I open my box of doom and tell them my darkestmemories,

I show them my deepest scars, and they leave,

Saying I deserve better.

I'm inside this box made of glass,
And everyone can see me,
Everyone can hear my screams,
I can't break the glass down,
I can't get out of it,
The air is getting thin and chilly,
And the heat is increasing,
I'm sweating and shivering all at once,
My hands are starting to shake,
My knees are giving in,
My body seems to be floating,
But at the same time, I'm being dragged in the ground,
Why is everyone laughing at me?
Why are they pointing fingers?
Why are some giving me the stink eye?
Why isn't anyone helping me?
~And then I opened my eyes,
oh, wait it was just another panic attack~

I think my waking hours are more haunting,
Than my nightmares will ever be.

Sometimes I feel like I'm playing a part in a story,

I have no say over,

It's a murder thriller and everyone is the killer,

But there is no corpse, no blood,

Just a dead heart in a living body.

My body is not a temple,

It is a museum,

Where there is history,

I do not want to repeat,

And there are memories,

I don't want anyone to touch.

My biggest critic is sometimes a bitch,
She tells me I am ugly,
She convinces me I am not good enough,
She makes me feel worthless,
She is sometimes mean,
She makes me believe the world is better off
withoutme,
My biggest critic?
~She stares at me through the mirror~

I wonder when,

A place will finally feel like home,

Because I'm tired of running,

I am tired of moving,

I am tired of living this lie,

That someday it will get better,

I am just tired of everything,

I. Am. Tired.

My mind is like a tornado,
A swirling vortex that goes around,
Collecting reasons,
To prove why I'll never be enough.

You don't truly escape self-harm's cruel spell,
Instead, you conceal the scars in art's gentle shell.

Do not place anyone on pedestals so high,

They only look down on you.

Everyone has a story,

everyone has something that has changed them,

But what right does it give them to hurt someone else?

I'm drunk on this pain,

I think I'm finally insane.

I would rather be a sad poem,

Than a forgotten footnote.

There's an essence to this existence,

That has never truly felt like mine.

I'm breaking again,
I don't know how to express in words,
It's like every time I say it, it just gets worse.

I find myself nestled on the sandy shore,
Gazing as the waves tenderly caress the land,
Wondering if the sea engages in playful dalliances with the shore,
Or perhaps it whispers tales of distant lands.

Your jokes were funny,

Only to you,

To me, they were my insecurities on display,

That you pointed out and laughed at.

I am a painting with the colors all muted,
The canvas fraying at the edges,
The strokes of my brush are fading,
But I promise there's depth within the layers.
I am a melody with the notes all blurred,
The sheet music creased and torn,
The harmonies are fading,
But I assure you, there's beauty in the melody.
I am a garden with the petals all wilted,
The soil dry and cracked,
The blooms are fading,
But beneath lies the promise of renewal and growth.
I am a star with the light dimming,
The sky obscured by clouds,
My shine may be fading,
But the radiance within still glimmers,
Waiting to be discovered

They say I need rescuing from the shadows,
That dance within,
But I stand firm, unyielding,
For this darkness is part of my essence,
If your love cannot embrace every facet of my being, Then don't let it touch me at all.

People have a habit of circling back into your life, When they realize the grass isn't greener on The other side,

They come knocking when the ones they thought were superior,

End up disappointing them,

Funny how they suddenly remember your worth,

When their illusions fade away.

And through the wounds, she healed,
But the scars still ached,
A suffering like no other, a void that will
never be filled,
She prayed to the devil,
For hell seemed less painful,
The Devil cried knowing there was more pain
in her Than hell could ever hold.

How many masks must I shed to feel like myself?
How many storms must I weather to be free?
How many doors must I shut to feel safe?
How many roots must I severe to taste vitality?

How many tears did you shed,
for who knew how to wield the dagger of betrayal?
How many broken pieces did you gather,
For the one who shattered you?
How many lies did you accept,
From the lips you couldn't help but kiss?
How many bruises did you bear,
For the one whose touch felt like both heaven and hell?
How many sacrifices did you make,
For the one who only knew how to take?
How many storms did you weather,
For the one who was the source of your chaos?
How many dreams did you surrender,
For the one who couldn't see your worth?
How many masks did you wear,
For the one who never truly saw you?
How many fears did you suppress,
For the one who was the cause of your anxieties?
How many boundaries did you erase,

For the one who only respected their own desires?

I cherished you like whispered secrets,
Known only to the moon and the night,
Hidden deep within the silence of my soul.

The lover in me is grieving,
The dreamer in me is weary,
The fighter in me is exhausted,
The wanderer in me is lost,
The optimist in me is fading,
The adventurer in me is restless,
The artist in me is uninspired,
The thinker in me is overwhelmed,
The believer in me is doubting,
The healer in me is wounded,
The leader in me is uncertain,
The rebel in me is subdued,
The builder in me is crumbling,
The child in me is forgotten,
The idealist in me is disillusioned,
The hero in me is defeated,

~Perhaps I'm just the person who fills the void~

Like the moon, my heart is adorned with countless stars, Yet it lingers shrouded in loneliness.

The deepest scars are often given by those you
blindly trust,
Leaving wounds that cut deeper than any
betrayal,
From a stranger ever could.
It's the sting of disbelief,
Accompanied by the realization,
That the very person you confided in,
The one you entrusted with your
vulnerabilities, and aspirations, Could be the
architect of your pain.

I believed the war had ended,

I started to breathe,

But when I opened my eyes,

I saw it was just the beginning.

I'm scared that one day I might not be sad anymore,
Like when I become the evil person I don't recognise.

*~The anxiety of being truly understood
surpasses my concern of being misunderstood
for the depth of connection it promises is worth
the vulnerability it demands ~*

Looking at myself from outside my body,
I see a soul drowning in a sea of despair,
A heart heavy with the burden of anxiety,
And eyes that have forgotten how to care.

I'm tired of always telling people how tired I am.
I just don't have the energy to share my feelings with Anyone else anymore.

Every time someone tells me they are okay,

A switch in my head turns on,

And I want to ask,

Are you okay okay,

Or are you okay that today you won't die.

And sometimes all you can do is cry under the blanket,

Close your eyes,

Sleep,

Wake up,

And continue living like nothing happened.

~Some people hold onto their pain to never hurt again~

How come we continually deceive ourselves,

Believing we've progressed?

Yet, the instant a trigger strikes,

All semblance shatters,

And the agony intensifies a hundredfold.

The weight of my secrets, a leaden cloak,
Dragging me down, until I choke,
Tainting my thoughts with its toxic oils,
Until my mind is no longer loyal.

Stress and anxiety grip me tight,
Sleep has failed me through the night,
Toss and turn, I count the sheep,
But rest remains a distant feat,
My mind races, my body tense,
Insomnia, my unwanted friend.

I've been running from everything for so long,
I don't know when to stop anymore.

Screams hidden behind pretty smiles,
Tears concealed behind hopeful eyes,
Pain unseen in loving hearts,
Dead souls masked within living bodies.

Different people know different versions of me,
The twisted part is, now I don't know which
version of me is the real me.

I've harbored a persistent fear of not being heard
That I ceased speaking entirely.

A cold realization weighs on me,
A truth I can now see,
We are all but a passing phase,
Easily replaced in a million ways,
A mere temporary thought, a whisper on the wind,
Easily forgotten, a memory thinned.

Is anyone truly happy?
Or do we all just hide behind masks,
Because deep down we all know,
That no one cares.

Sometimes I feel like I'm looking at myself,
from the outside,
And I am just disappointed at what I see,
Like I'm trapped in a world from which I will
never be free.

It's not that I cannot swim,
But I simply stopped trying,
Which resulted in me sinking into the depths
of my sorrow,
A place I wouldn't want anyone to go to.

I want to breathe,
Without feeling guilty about living,
I want to smile,
Without the fear of something bad waiting to happen,
I want to live,
Without hating myself everyday.

I'm sure god has a list of favorites,
And I'm beginning to think,
I'm nowhere on it.

Tell me about yourself they say,
I look at them confused,
Which self do I tell them of?
Which self do I tell them of?
The one with shattered dreams,
The one with silent screams,
Or the one drowning in tears?
Do you want to hear about the battles lost,
Or the scars I carry at any cost?
Should I speak of the darkness within,
Or the loneliness that's always been?
The one that hides behind a smile,
Concealing a heartache that stretches for miles,
Or the one that bears the weight of regret,
And the memories I'd rather forget?
Shall I recount the moments of despair,
Or the echoes of laughter no longer there?
Should I share the pieces of a broken soul,
Or the emptiness that takes its toll?
My story is a tragic symphony,
With melodies of pain and agony,
Each strain echoes the price of loss.

So when you ask about myself, you see,

It's not just one, but many versions of me.

The chains in my mind,
Have kept me from moving,
But I don't breakout of them,
Because I don't know where to go once I'm free.

I think I am in love with this darkness,

For when you sit in it for so long,

That's all you can do,

Just accept it.

I'm dreaming with my eyes wide open,

But they seem to be nightmares too.

My mind is a judgment house,
Where I'm the accused on trial,
And in this courtroom,
Every thought is a prosecutor,
Every memory is a piece of evidence,
Every tear is a silent witness,
Every heartbeat is a painful reminder,
Every smile a fragile facade,
Every laugh a hollow echo,
Every dream a fading illusion,
Every touch a distant memory,
Every word is a sharp blade,
Every night a battleground,
Every morning a weary surrender,
Every breath is a struggle,
Every hope is a cruel illusion.

Everybody is talking and no one is listening,
So many voices but nothing good to say.

I stopped chasing other shadows for shelter, realizing I often wandered in the darkness of my own uncertainty.

I don't want to fight for a place anymore,

I just want to feel like I belong.

I feel like my life is slipping by,

Every moment lost is a weight upon my soul,

Dragging me closer to a fate I cannot escape.

~The memories of better days have faded into the abyss of forgotten yesterdays~

Sometimes I wish to wake up,
In a mind that's calm,
In a mood that's consistent,
In a soul that's unscathed,
In a body that's not mine,
In a time when I was still a child,
For she knew what life was,
While I romanticize death.

In fleeting hours, I wrestle with you love's
elusive grasp,
A sense of unworthiness clouding my path,
And I silently retreat and wander through
solitude'sdomain,
Seeking solace in the vacant corridors of my
mind's terrain,
Where amidst shadows cast,
I spin intricate tapestries of memories past,
Yearning to fill the voids left by absence's
sting,
I dwell in the realm where imagined echoes
sing.

How many battles have you fought,
Since the day you were hurt?
How many days have you stayed up late,
From the nightmares of their doing?
How many hours have you spent,
Wondering 'What could I have done to stop the abuse?'
How many lifetimes have you contemplated,
That all that happened was your fault?

Sometimes I think I wanted all this pain,
To justify the sadness filled in me.

Imagine every morning you wake up,
Pondering whether it will be a day of "I'll get through just today,"
Or "I'm going to enjoy today,"
It's exhausting.

Pain is often described as an inherent aspect of existence,
Yet there are moments when it seems to encompass my entire existence.

~I'm carrying dead weight of people's words in my head~

When the inevitable storm of disillusionment arrives,
It sweeps away my illusions,
Leaving behind shards of shattered dreams.

My saddest words are not the ones I left unspoken,
But those I whispered softly to an empty room.

I harbor a fear of being abandoned by my
own shadow,
Like a reminder of lost souls who've left me to
wade in sorrow's undertow.

~The bustling cities can never rival the cacophony within my mind~

If i were to write a horror story,
I would simply write down all of my regrets,
and see my fears come alive.

My house isn't made of glass,
But I am, in a way,
Transparent, vulnerable,
In the light of day.
You see through my walls,
Into my soul's deep hues,
Every crack and fracture,
All my hidden clues.
Every word spoken, every sigh,
Echoes through the halls of my mind,
I may not shatter with a single blow,
But inside, I can feel the cracks grow.

~Nobody should ever feel compelled to carry the weight of existence~

I am afraid to bleed into the pain I've been holding for years,
What if it isn't enough to end the hurting?
Will my tears mix with the crimson stain,
And wash away the torment,
The silent disdain?
But what if my sorrow runs deeper than skin,
A cavern of sorrow where no light can get in,
I fear the ache will linger,
Refusing to depart,
A haunting melody echoing within my heart.

I was a shipwrecked sailor,
Stranded on the shore,
While you stormed in like a raging tempest,
Berating me for the taste of salt on my lips.

Acknowledgements

First and foremost, I would like to thank my Parents and siblings, and people I truly care for, for their unwavering support, encouragement, and inspiration. Your love and belief in me have been my driving force, and I am forever grateful for your presence in my life.

To my Sister, thank you for encouraging me to write down every thought my muddled mind came up with

To the poets whose work has influenced mine, thank you for your artistry, your wisdom, and your vision. Your words have touched my soul and helped me find my own voice.

Lastly, I would like to acknowledge my readers, for taking the time to engage with my poems and for allowing my words to resonate with you. It is an honor to be able to connect with you through poetry, and I hope that my words have brought you some comfort, joy, or inspiration. Thank you all for being a part of this journey with me.

About the author

In the quiet depths of the night, where the world dims and the mind wander freely, there exists an author whose words dance in the shadows and whisper secrets beneath the stars.

With a pen in hand and a mind full of dreams, the author's journey into the realm of storytelling began at a young age of twelve. Drawing from a wellspring of experiences and emotions, the author infuses their writing with depth, sincerity, and a touch of whimsy. Each word carefully chosen, each sentence crafted with care, they invite readers to delve into the recesses of their imagination and explore the myriad possibilities that lie within.

"Midnight Thoughts" serves as a window into the author's inner world, a collection of musings born from the quietude of the night. Through prose and poetry, they explore themes of love, loss, hope, and longing, inviting readers to ponder life's mysteries under the gentle glow of the moon.